40
FASCINATING
PLACES
OF THE
BIBLE

40
FASCINATING
PLACES
OF THE
BIBLE

Ellen Caughey

BARBOUR
PUBLISHING

ISBN 978-1-60260-021-8

Published by Barbour Publishing, Inc., P.O. Box 719, Uhrichsville, Ohio 44683, www.barbourbooks.com

Our mission is to publish and distribute inspirational products offering exceptional value and biblical encouragement to the masses.

Member of the
Evangelical Christian
Publishers Association

Contents

Introduction

Get to know the key places of God's Word, and you'll better understand the great characters, stories, and teachings of scripture. That's the idea behind *40 Fascinating Places of the Bible*.

Every biblical man and woman lived in the context of a *place*—lands of towns and cities, hills and valleys, rivers, deserts, forests, or lakes. The stories we remember—of Moses' miracles, Daniel's courage, Jesus' teachings, and Paul's missionary work—occurred in real places, full of real people. The more we know of those places, the more clearly we can see how those stories unfolded, and what they mean to us today.

In this little book, you'll find brief accounts of forty of the most prominent places of scripture. Every entry follows this outline:

- NAME/MEANING
- WHERE IN THE WORLD?
- WHERE IN THE BIBLE?
- WHAT HAPPENED THERE?
- WHAT'S UP TODAY?
- WHAT'S IN IT FOR ME?

Enjoy this guided tour of *40 Fascinating Places of the Bible*!

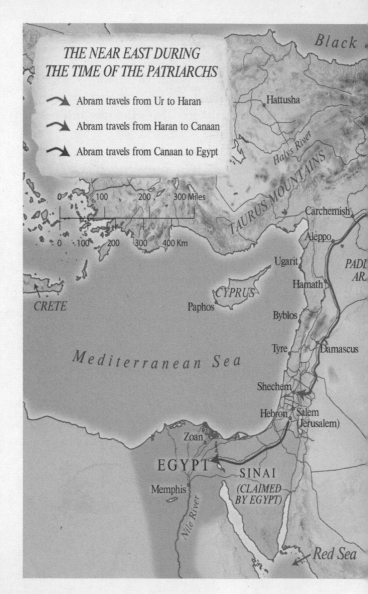

THE NEAR EAST DURING THE TIME OF THE PATRIARCHS

- Abram travels from Ur to Haran
- Abram travels from Haran to Canaan
- Abram travels from Canaan to Egypt

Black

Hattusha

Halys River

TAURUS MOUNTAINS

0   100   200   300 Miles

0   100   200   300   400 Km

Carchemish

Aleppo

Ugarit

PADI AR.

Hamath

CRETE

CYPRUS

Paphos

Byblos

Mediterranean Sea

Tyre

Damascus

Shechem

Hebron   Salem
          (Jerusalem)

Zoan

EGYPT

SINAI
(CLAIMED
BY EGYPT)

Memphis

Nile River

Red Sea

Caspian Sea

ARARAT

Rages

Nineveh

ASSYRIA

Asshur

ZAGROS MOUNTAINS

Mari

Tigris River

Euphrates River

MARI

Susa

Babylon

ELAM

BABYLONIA

ABIAN
SERT'

Ur

Persian Gulf

Dumah

N

Copyright © 2007 by Barbour Publishing, Inc.

Tema

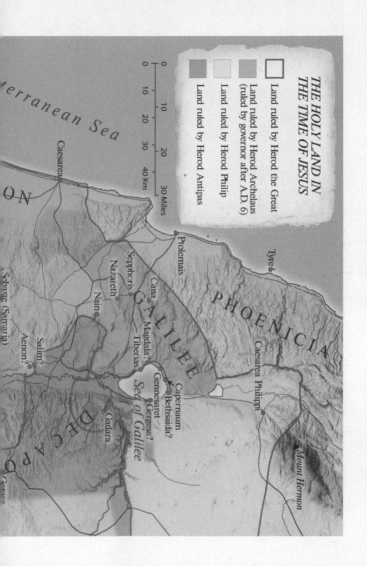

THE HOLY LAND IN
THE TIME OF JESUS

Land ruled by Herod the Great

Land ruled by Herod Archelaus
(ruled by governor after A.D. 6)

Land ruled by Herod Philip

Land ruled by Herod Antipas

0   10   20   30   40 Km

0   10   20   30 Miles

Mediterranean Sea

Caesarea

Ptolemais

Tyre

PHOENICIA

Caesarea Philippi

Mount Hermon

Sepphoris

Nazareth

Cana

GALILEE

Nain

Magdala?

Tiberias

Gennesaret

Capernaum

Bethsaida?

Gergesa?

Sea of Galilee

Salim?

Aenon?

Sebaste (Samaria)

DECAPOLIS

Gadara

THE ROMAN EMPIRE IN
THE TIME OF PAUL

GERMANIA

*Atlantic
Ocean*

GAUL

ITAL

Rome

HISPANIA
(SPAIN)

Cordoba

Carthage

MAURETANIA   NUMIDIA

S A H

| 0 | 250 | 500 | 750 | 1000 mi |

| 0 | 500 | 1000 | 1500 km |

Antioch

NAME/MEANING
"Named in Honor of Antiochus"

WHERE IN THE WORLD?
The town of Antakya in southern Turkey is situated on the site of ancient Antioch. Antakya is twenty miles from the Mediterranean Sea, twelve miles from the Syrian border, and located on the eastern bank of the Orontes River.

WHERE IN THE BIBLE?
"And the disciples were called Christians first in Antioch" (Acts 11:26 KJV).

WHAT HAPPENED THERE?
Founded in 300 BC, Antioch became a bustling metropolis of a half million during the Hellenistic Age and, later, a thriving center of Christendom in the Roman Empire. In fact, the apostle Paul and Barnabas were called by the Holy Spirit in Antioch, which served as the starting point of Paul's first missionary journey. Succeeding centuries were not kind to Antioch. In the fifth century, the city suffered a massive earthquake, killing a quarter million people. Antioch was later conquered by the Arabs and besieged during the Crusades. Antakya was part of the French Protectorate of Syria until 1939, when it was officially annexed by the Republic of Turkey.

What's Up Today?

Antakya (population 144,000) is primarily a destination for those interested in ancient Roman and Byzantine mosaics. Of special note are the Hatay Archaeological Museum and the Cave Church of St. Peter, which was declared a holy site by the Vatican in 1983. Little of the ancient city of Antioch has been uncovered—it's believed that most of the ruins lie buried under the Orontes River.

What's in It for Me?

If you call yourself a Christian, you have something in common with ancient Antioch. That's where members of the early church coined that name—a name that has stood the test of time.

Ararat

NAME/MEANING

The Hebrew Torah recorded the name as "Rrt," which scholars believe to represent Urartu, a civilization destroyed by the Medes in the sixth century BC. More recent names for the mountain, given by Turks and Kurds, respectively, translate as "Mountain of Pain" and "Mountain of Fire," referring to its volcanic activity.

WHERE IN THE WORLD?

At 16,854 feet, Ararat is the tallest peak in Turkey. Located in the northeast corner of Turkey, Ararat is ten miles west of Iran and twenty miles south of Armenia.

WHERE IN THE BIBLE?

"And the ark rested in the seventh month, on the seventeenth day of the month, upon the mountains of Ararat" (Genesis 8:4 KJV).

WHAT HAPPENED THERE?

In the centuries following the landing of Noah's ark, Ararat and its surrounding area were hotly contested. Previously ruled over by Armenians, Romans, Persians, Mongols, Ottomans, and Russians, after World War I Ararat was considered part of the Democratic Republic of Armenia. However, since the Treaty of Kars in 1923, Ararat has been considered part of Turkey, though it remains the national symbol of Armenia.

WHAT'S UP TODAY?

Explorers, geologists, and Bible scholars continue to scour Ararat and the immediate vicinity for the remains of Noah's ark. Since 2001, when the government of Turkey reopened Ararat to climbers, three areas have been the focus of interest: the Ararat anomaly, a darkened area on the top of the mountain; Durupinar, eighteen miles south of the summit; and the Ahora Gorge, another area on the mountain. Along with numerous hoaxes, there have been reputable reports over the years of an arklike structure resting on the mountain.

WHAT'S IN IT FOR ME?

Ararat will always be associated with Noah. For Christians, Noah is a powerful reminder of what happens when we trust God completely.

Areopagus

NAME/MEANING

Areopagus (or Areios Pagos) means "Hill of Ares," referring to the Greek god said to be tried on this hill for the murder of Poseidon's son Alirrothios. The Bible refers to Areopagus as "Mars' Hill."

WHERE IN THE WORLD?

Areopagus is a rocky hill (370 feet high) located northwest of the Acropolis in Athens, Greece.

WHERE IN THE BIBLE?

"And they took him, and brought him unto Areopagus, saying, May we know what this new doctrine, whereof thou speakest, is?" (Acts 17:19 KJV).

"Paul then stood up in the meeting of the Areopagus and said: 'Men of Athens! I see that in every way you are very religious. For as I walked around and looked carefully at your objects of worship, I even found an altar with this inscription: TO AN UNKNOWN GOD. Now what you worship as something unknown I am going to proclaim to you" (Acts 17:22–23 NIV).

What Happened There?

Areopagus was the site where the ancient Greek council of elders met to govern and, later, to conduct criminal trials. During Roman rule, the Areopagus, another name for this council, continued to function as it had before. It drew particular attention as the site of an altar "To an Unknown God." While awaiting the arrival of Silas and Timothy in Athens, Paul was taken to the Areopagus, where he proceeded to explain the identity of his God. "The God who made the world and everything in it is the Lord of heaven and earth and does not live in temples built by hands" (Acts 17:24 NIV).

What's Up Today?

Visitors to the Areopagus can climb the rocky mount, just as Paul did, and be rewarded with a spectacular vista of modern-day Greece.

What's in It for Me?

The apostle Paul's words at the Areopagus remind us that there can be no other gods—we know we serve the risen Savior!

Athens

NAME/MEANING
Named after the Greek goddess Athena

WHERE IN THE WORLD?
Athens, the largest city and capital of Greece (metro population more than three million), is located in the Attica periphery of central Greece.

WHERE IN THE BIBLE?
"And they that conducted Paul brought him unto Athens: and receiving a commandment unto Silas and Timotheus for to come to him with all speed, they departed" (Acts 17:15 KJV).

"Then Paul stood in the midst of Mars' hill, and said, Ye men of Athens, I perceive that in all things ye are too superstitious" (Acts 17:22 KJV).

WHAT HAPPENED THERE?
Although Athens has been inhabited for three thousand years, its golden age was during the first millennium BC as the powerful city-state of ancient Greece. Acclaimed as a center for the arts, philosophy, and learning, it was the home of the schools of both Plato and Aristotle. By the fifth century BC, Athens had become known as the cradle of civilization and the birthplace of democracy, symbolized by the landmark structure of the Parthenon, still visible today atop the

Acropolis. Subsequently conquered and occupied by Rome, and later part of the Byzantine and Ottoman empires, Athens did not become known as the capital of Greece until 1833. Athens experienced a period of growth following the Greco-Turkish War of 1919–22, only to see its fortunes suffer during the Nazi occupation of World War II. Athens was host to the first modern-day Olympic Games in 1896, as well as the Summer Games of 2004.

WHAT'S UP TODAY?
Athens is the eighth-largest capital of Europe and a bustling center of commerce and tourism. Following the 2004 Games, with the addition of a new airport and improvement of the city's air quality, Athens has once again become a popular destination.

WHAT'S IN IT FOR ME?
Great civilizations come and go, but those who trust in Jesus Christ will live forever.

Babylon

NAME/MEANING
From the Akkadian *Babilu*, meaning "Gateway of the Gods"

WHERE IN THE WORLD?
The ruins of Babylon can be found in modern-day Iraq, in Babil province just outside the city of Hilla, about fifty miles south of Baghdad.

WHERE IN THE BIBLE?
"Behold, the days come, that all that is in thine house, and that which thy fathers have laid up in store unto this day, shall be carried into Babylon: nothing shall be left, saith the LORD" (2 Kings 20:17 KJV).

"By the rivers of Babylon we sat and wept when we remembered Zion" (Psalm 137:1 NIV).

"And this whole land shall be a desolation, and an astonishment; and these nations shall serve the king of Babylon seventy years" (Jeremiah 25:11 KJV).

"And Babylon, the glory of kingdoms, the beauty of the Chaldees' excellency, shall be as when God overthrew Sodom and Gomorrah" (Isaiah 13:19 KJV).

What Happened There?

Babylon, built on both sides of the Euphrates River, dates beyond the twentieth century BC. The city was razed by Sennacherib and the Assyrians in 689 BC, but rebuilt shortly afterward. Under Nebuchadnezzar II (605–562 BC) Babylon gained a reputation for being one of the wonders of the world, famous for its Ishtar Gate, hanging gardens, and ziggurat. During that same period, Babylon attacked Jerusalem (602 BC), taking many Israelites captive for what would be known as the seventy-year Babylonian captivity. In 539 BC Babylon fell to the Persians and then in 331 BC to Alexander the Great. By 141 BC, Babylon was desolate, its inhabitants dispersed.

What's Up Today?

Former Iraqi president Saddam Hussein began to restore Babylon to its former glory in 1985. After he was deposed, the project halted. More recently, Iraqi and United Nations officials have been discussing plans to turn Babylon into a theme park and cultural center.

What's in It for Me?

Biblical prophecies about Babylon remind us that God's Word is always true, throughout all the ages.

Bethlehem

NAME/MEANING
From the Hebrew *Beit Lehem*, meaning "House of Bread"

WHERE IN THE WORLD?
Bethlehem is located on the West Bank, in a Palestinian-controlled area between Israel and Jordan to the north of the Dead Sea. Bethlehem is six miles south of the Old City of Jerusalem.

WHERE IN THE BIBLE?
"And Rachel died, and was buried in the way to Ephrath, which is Bethlehem" (Genesis 35:19 KJV).

"So Naomi returned, and Ruth the Moabitess, her daughter in law. . .to Bethlehem in the beginning of barley harvest" (Ruth 1:22 KJV).

"Fill thine horn with oil, and go, I will send thee to Jesse the Bethlehemite: for I have provided me a king among his sons" (1 Samuel 16:1 KJV).

"And thou Bethlehem, in the land of Juda, art not the least among the princes of Juda: for out of thee shall come a Governor, that shall rule my people Israel" (Matthew 2:6 KJV).

WHAT HAPPENED THERE?

The Bible states that Rachel was buried near Bethlehem and also that Naomi, Ruth and Boaz, and their grandson, Jesse, would all call Bethlehem home. The most important event was Jesus' birth, proclaimed by angels, shepherds, and wise men. Although Bethlehem was destroyed during Simon Bar-Kokhba's revolt against Rome (AD 132–135), the town was resurrected by the Romans, who set up a shrine to Adonis on the site of the Nativity. The first Christian church in Bethlehem was constructed in AD 326, and the town enjoyed continued prosperity during the Crusades. Although much of Bethlehem was again destroyed by the Ottomans, recent history has seen Bethlehem revered as a holy city.

WHAT'S UP TODAY?

On December 21, 1995, Bethlehem came under rule of the Palestinian Authority, which has limited the number of pilgrims visiting the city. Visitors must submit to rigorous screening to enter the area. Currently, more Muslims than Christians reside in Bethlehem.

WHAT'S IN IT FOR ME?

Jesus was born in Bethlehem—but He'll live in our hearts when we ask Him.

Cana

NAME/MEANING
Possibly "Reedy"

WHERE IN THE WORLD?
There is a modern village in Israel called Cana, but the most likely site of the biblical Cana is either Kefr Kana, four miles northeast of Nazareth, or Khirbet Kana, a village nine miles north of Nazareth.

WHERE IN THE BIBLE?
"There was a marriage in Cana of Galilee; and the mother of Jesus was there: and both Jesus was called, and his disciples, to the marriage" (John 2:1–2 KJV).

"This beginning of miracles did Jesus in Cana of Galilee, and manifested forth his glory; and his disciples believed on him" (John 2:11 KJV).

"So Jesus came again into Cana of Galilee. . . . And there was a certain nobleman, whose son was sick at Capernaum" (John 4:46 KJV).

WHAT HAPPENED THERE?
Jesus' first miracle occurred at a wedding in Cana, when His mother, Mary, informed Him there was no more wine. In view of His disciples, Jesus ordered the servants to fill some large pots with water. When the ruler present tasted the water that Jesus had miraculously

changed, he was astounded that the bridegroom had saved the best wine for last. Shortly afterward Jesus returned to Cana where He met a nobleman who said that his son was sick. Instead of visiting the boy, Jesus told the nobleman to go since his son had been healed. The Bible notes in an account following Jesus' resurrection that one of Jesus' disciples, Nathanael, was from Cana. So the town of Cana is associated with the beginning and end of Jesus' ministry on earth.

WHAT'S UP TODAY?

Archaeological digs continue at both sites reputed to be the Cana of the Bible. Roman jars and other relics from the time of Jesus have been found at both locations.

WHAT'S IN IT FOR ME?

Jesus' disciples witnessed His miracle at Cana and believed. Can you believe in Jesus without a miracle?

Capernaum

NAME/MEANING
"City of Consolation" or "Village of Nahum"

WHERE IN THE WORLD?
The ruins of Capernaum are located on the northwest shore of the Sea of Galilee, approximately two and a half miles from the town of Bethsaida.

WHERE IN THE BIBLE?
"Leaving Nazareth, he [Jesus] went and lived in Capernaum, which was by the lake in the area of Zebulun and Naphtali" (Matthew 4:13 NIV).

" 'And you, Capernaum, will you be lifted up to the skies? No, you will go down to the depths'" (Luke 10:15 NIV).

"When evening came, his disciples went down to the lake, where they got into a boat and set off across the lake for Capernaum" (John 6:16–17 NIV).

WHAT HAPPENED THERE?
Capernaum was a small fishing village (population one thousand to fifteen hundred) in existence from the second century BC to approximately the eleventh century AD. Primarily known as the city where Jesus made His home after leaving Nazareth, Capernaum was also home to the disciples Peter, Andrew, James, and John. While in Capernaum, Jesus healed the servant of

an influential centurion and also spoke of Himself as the "bread of life" in the small synagogue (John 6:35). In Capernaum Jesus also cured Peter's mother-in-law of a fever (Matthew 8:14–15); healed a man with palsy let down through the roof (Matthew 9:1–8); and raised Jairus's daughter from the dead (Matthew 9:18–26). Despite all these miracles, Capernaum showed a lack of faith that drew Jesus' condemnation (Luke 10:15).

WHAT'S UP TODAY?

During the nineteenth century, geographers identified the ruins and the synagogue. Since 1894 when a portion of the site was purchased by the Franciscan Custody of the Holy Land, excavations have continued, revealing what may be Peter's home.

WHAT'S IN IT FOR ME?

The people of Capernaum knew about Jesus, but many did not accept Him as God's Son. Do you know *about* Him, or do you *know* Him?

Corinth

NAME/MEANING
From the Greek *Corinthos*, meaning "Descendant of Greek God Helios [the Sun]"

WHERE IN THE WORLD?
Corinth, forty-eight miles southwest of Athens, is situated on the Isthmus of Corinth, a narrow strip of land that connects Peloponnese with northern Greece.

WHERE IN THE BIBLE?
"After this, Paul left Athens and went to Corinth. There he met a Jew named Aquila. . .with his wife Priscilla" (Acts 18:1–2 NIV).

"While Apollos was at Corinth, Paul took the road through the interior and arrived at Ephesus" (Acts 19:1 NIV).

WHAT HAPPENED THERE?
Although Corinth was first settled and destroyed during the prehistoric era, the city, with its great temple dedicated to Aphrodite, was considered among the most desirable during the Classical age. Destroyed in 146 BC, Corinth was rebuilt by Julius Caesar in 44 BC. When the apostle Paul lived in Corinth (AD 51–52), the city was the capital of Roman Greece, with a population of eight hundred thousand. Following his time in Corinth working as a tentmaker, Paul wrote two epistles to the

Christian church there. Corinth, which was destroyed by earthquakes in AD 375 and 551, later regained some of its luster when it became a sought-after prize during the Crusades. After being controlled by the Turks and the Venetians, Corinth became part of Greece in the early nineteenth century, losing out to Athens as capital city in 1833.

WHAT'S UP TODAY?

After the completion of the Corinth Canal in 1893, which created a shipping route between the Ionian and Aegean seas, Corinth developed as an industrial center connecting northern and southern Greece. Today a city of some thirty thousand, Corinth is still tied to its past with ongoing archaeological digs and fairly well-preserved ruins, mostly from the Roman era.

WHAT'S IN IT FOR ME?

It was in Corinth that God gave the apostle Paul a message that applies to us, too: "Do not be afraid; keep on speaking, do not be silent" (Acts 18:9 NIV).

Damascus

NAME/MEANING
From *Damashaq* or *Dimashq*, which could denote a fast-moving camel, to indicate the swift building of the city, or the great-great-grandson of Noah; in Arabic the city is known as *As-sham*, meaning "Northern."

WHERE IN THE WORLD?
Damascus, the capital of Syria, is located approximately fifty miles from the Mediterranean Sea, on a plateau bordered by the Anti-Lebanon Mountains.

WHERE IN THE BIBLE?
"During the night Abram divided his men to attack them. . .pursuing them as far as Hobah, north of Damascus" (Genesis 14:15 NIV).

"As he neared Damascus on his journey, suddenly a light from heaven flashed around him. He fell to the ground and heard a voice say to him, 'Saul, Saul, why do you persecute me?'" (Acts 9:3–4 NIV).

WHAT HAPPENED THERE?
Damascus, which traces its history to 10,000 BC, is one of the oldest continuously inhabited cities in the world. In fact, the book of Genesis mentions the existence of Damascus during Abraham's time. During an occupation by the Arameans, Damascus came to prominence, especially during the rule of Ben-Hadad

around 1100 BC, a reign mentioned by the prophets Jeremiah and Amos. Conquered by the Assyrians under Tiglath-Pileser III in 732 BC, Babylon under Nebuchadnezzar in 572 BC, Persia in 538 BC, and Rome in 64 BC, Damascus was a highly contested metropolis. During the Roman occupation, the apostle Paul, then known as Saul, a well-known persecutor of Christians, was struck blind by God as he approached the city with plans to arrest believers. Following the Roman occupation, Damascus became part of the Muslim empire—and under Saladin became capital of Egypt in the AD 1150s. Later, Damascus was controlled by the Ottomans for four hundred years, beginning in the early 1500s. More recently, in 1920, the French made Damascus capital of the League of Nations mandate of Syria. In 1946 Syria gained full independence.

WHAT'S UP TODAY?
Damascus (population approximately two million), a predominantly Sunni Muslim city that boasts ancient ruins and modern universities, has experienced unrest due to Middle Eastern conflicts.

WHAT'S IN IT FOR ME?
The story of Saul on his way to Damascus shows us that *anyone*—no matter what their past—can become a new person in Christ Jesus.

Dead Sea

NAME/MEANING
"Sea of Salt"

WHERE IN THE WORLD?
The Dead Sea lies between Israel to the west and Jordan to the east, just south of Jericho. The Jordan River flows into the Dead Sea.

WHERE IN THE BIBLE?
"All these latter kings joined forces in the Valley of Siddim (the Salt Sea)" (Genesis 14:3 NIV).

" 'For your eastern boundary [of Canaan]...the boundary will go down along the Jordan and end at the Salt Sea'" (Numbers 34:10, 12 NIV).

"While the water flowing down to the Sea of the Arabah (the Salt Sea) was completely cut off. So the people crossed over opposite Jericho" (Joshua 3:16 NIV).

WHAT HAPPENED THERE?
The Bible, which refers to the body of water as the Salt Sea, records several events. In the book of Genesis, the "War of the Kings" of Abram's day occurred by the Dead Sea. Because of the proximity of Sodom and Gomorrah, many believe that their charred remains were consumed by the Dead Sea. And, very importantly, God used the Dead Sea as a boundary for the land of

Canaan. The Jewish stronghold of Masada was built on the western banks of the Dead Sea, and the area around the sea was also the site of several Greek Orthodox monasteries. From 1947 to 1956, in eleven caves on the northwest shore of the Dead Sea, the Dead Sea Scrolls were discovered. Many of these scrolls were ancient texts from the Hebrew Bible.

WHAT'S UP TODAY?

At 1,378 feet below sea level, the Dead Sea is one of the lowest points on earth. Because of its location and chemical makeup, the Dead Sea has been a center of health research and industrial exploitation. While Bedouins have lived in the area for centuries, the Dead Sea has also become a magnet for tourists.

WHAT'S IN IT FOR ME?

Like the ancient Israelites moving into their "Promised Land," God has given us boundaries, too. . .boundaries that give us the best quality of life.

Eden, Garden of

NAME/MEANING
From the Hebrew, meaning "Pleasantness" or "Delight"

WHERE IN THE WORLD?
The Garden of Eden was located near the confluence of four rivers, two of which are the Tigris and Euphrates. The other two—the Pishon and Gihon—are unknown today. If the Garden were located at the source of the Tigris and Euphrates, that would put it in eastern Turkey. From the dried beds of what may have been the Pishon and Gihon, some scholars guess that the Garden was more likely in the Tigris-Euphrates Valley, about 150 miles north of the Persian Gulf.

WHERE IN THE BIBLE?
"Now the LORD God had planted a garden in the east, in Eden; and there he put the man he had formed" (Genesis 2:8 NIV).

"A river watering the garden flowed from Eden; from there it was separated into four headwaters" (Genesis 2:10 NIV).

"So the LORD God banished him from the Garden of Eden to work the ground from which he had been taken. After he drove the man out, he placed on the east side of the Garden of Eden cherubim and a flaming sword flashing back and forth to guard the way to the tree of life" (Genesis 3:23–24 NIV).

WHAT HAPPENED THERE?

Eden was the name of the place God created as a beautiful, lush garden—the home of the first man and woman, Adam and Eve. When they ate a forbidden fruit from the "tree of the knowledge of good and evil," they were banished from the garden forever.

WHAT'S UP TODAY?

The Garden of Eden has never been found.

WHAT'S IN IT FOR ME?

Ever since Adam and Eve were expelled from the Garden of Eden, the days of our human lives have been numbered. With that in mind, let's live every day for Jesus.

Egypt

NAME/MEANING
From ancient texts, the name meant "Black Land"; the modern name, Egypt, means "The Two Straits."

WHERE IN THE WORLD?
Egypt is located in northern Africa, with Libya to the west, Sudan to the south, Israel to the east, and the Mediterranean Sea to the north.

WHERE IN THE BIBLE?
"And they took their cattle, and their goods, which they had gotten in the land of Canaan, and came into Egypt, Jacob, and all his seed with him" (Genesis 46:6 KJV).

"But Moses said to God, 'Who am I, that I should go to Pharaoh and bring the Israelites out of Egypt?'" (Exodus 3:11 NIV).

"The angel of the Lord appeareth to Joseph in a dream, saying, Arise, and take the young child and his mother, and flee into Egypt" (Matthew 2:13 KJV).

WHAT HAPPENED THERE?
The land became populated as early as 10,000 BC due to the fertile Nile Valley. By 3000 BC, the famous dynasties, those that built the pyramids and the Sphinx, were in control. But by 343 BC, when Egypt fell to the Persians (who were followed by the Greeks and Romans), the

glory of ancient Egypt was over. The Bible records Abram's two visits to Egypt, as well as Joseph's rise to power there and the ultimate captivity of the Hebrews under Pharaoh before their dramatic rescue by God through the Red Sea. Mary, Joseph, and baby Jesus settled in Egypt for a time to avoid the murderous King Herod. Tradition says that the biblical Mark brought Christianity to Egypt, and the Egyptian Coptic Church was founded after AD 451. By AD 639, the land was invaded by Muslim Arabs, to be followed by the Ottomans in 1517. Britain's declared protectorate over Egypt in 1914 would be the last foreign domination. In 1922 Egypt declared its independence from Britain and became a republic in 1953.

WHAT'S UP TODAY?
Egypt is the second largest country in Africa, with Cairo as its capital and largest city. The vast majority of the population is Muslim, and religious toleration has come under attack in recent years. Despite the 1978 Camp David Accords signed by then president Anwar Sadat, tension still exists between Egypt and Israel after the Six-Day War of 1967 and the Yom Kippur War of October 1973.

WHAT'S IN IT FOR ME?
On their flight to Egypt, Mary and Joseph may have seen the pyramids, the only one of the Seven Wonders of the Ancient World still standing. What will outlast the pyramids? God's Word (see Psalm 119:89).

En Gedi

NAME/MEANING
From the Hebrew "Kid [Goat] Spring" or "Of the Kid"

WHERE IN THE WORLD?
En Gedi is the largest freshwater oasis located on the western shore of the Dead Sea. The oasis is on the eastern edge of the Judean Desert and is approximately thirty-five miles southeast of Jerusalem.

WHERE IN THE BIBLE?
"After Saul returned from pursuing the Philistines, he was told, 'David is in the Desert of En Gedi'" (1 Samuel 24:1 NIV).

"My lover is to me a cluster of henna blossoms from the vineyards of En Gedi" (Song of Songs 1:14 NIV).

" 'Fishermen will stand along the shore; from En Gedi to En Eglaim there will be places for spreading nets'" (Ezekiel 47:10 NIV).

WHAT HAPPENED THERE?
En Gedi can be traced to the Chalcolithic Period (4000–3150 BC), primarily because of the ruins of a temple located near the oasis. In the Bible, the jealous King Saul pursued David to En Gedi, intent on killing the popular young warrior. At one point, when Saul took refuge in a cave of En Gedi, David was close

enough to take the king's life—but instead only cut off a piece of Saul's robe. En Gedi has been home to Jewish settlers, starting in the seventh century BC and ending around AD 500.

WHAT'S UP TODAY?

En Gedi and the surrounding area are part of En Gedi National Park, which was founded in 1972 and is considered one of the most important ecological reserves of Israel. Because four springs feed into the oasis, the area is known for its lush ecosystem and its diverse wildlife. Today the Israeli kibbutz, or communal farm, of En Gedi is located one kilometer from the oasis, on the shores of the spring called Nahal Arugot.

WHAT'S IN IT FOR ME?

David found refuge in En Gedi. We can find ours in Jesus.

Ephesus

NAME/MEANING

From *Apasas*, which meant "City of the Mother Goddess," in reference to the legend that Ephesus was founded by female warriors.

WHERE IN THE WORLD?

The ruins of Ephesus are located in western Turkey, near the city of Selcuk, six miles from the Aegean Sea.

WHERE IN THE BIBLE?

"They arrived at Ephesus, where Paul left Priscilla and Aquila. He himself went into the synagogue and reasoned with the Jews" (Acts 18:19 NIV).

" 'To the angel of the church in Ephesus write. . . Yet I hold this against you: You have forsaken your first love'" (Revelation 2:1, 4 NIV).

WHAT HAPPENED THERE?

First settled in the tenth century BC, Ephesus was in turn conquered by the Lydians, Persians, Greeks, and Romans. The city boasted one of the Seven Wonders of the Ancient World, the Temple of Artemis, as well as an outdoor theatre that hosted gladiators, a sophisticated aqueduct system, and the Library of Celsus. During the Roman era, Ephesus was the capital of proconsular Asia and a center of trade and commerce, with a population around a half million. When the apostle

Paul lived there (AD 65–68), he wrote his first epistle to the Corinthians. Paul's tenure in Ephesus was marked by his dispute with the artisans in the temple, who made their living selling likenesses of the goddess Diana. A riot broke out, led by a silversmith named Demetrius, who convinced the artisans that Paul was a threat to their business. It is widely believed that the apostle John spent his final years in Ephesus, where he also cared for Jesus' mother, Mary. John was directed by God to address one of the seven letters of the book of Revelation to the church in Ephesus. Although the city was sacked by the Goths in AD 263, Ephesus enjoyed some importance within the Byzantine Empire. After Arabs sacked the city in AD 700 and 716 and the harbor filled with silt from the Kaystros River, Ephesus never recovered its former grandeur. It was finally abandoned during the fifteenth century.

WHAT'S UP TODAY?

Visitors to the ruins of Ephesus are rewarded with glimpses of the Library of Celsus, the theatre, and one remaining column of the Temple of Artemis—as well as what may be the house belonging to Mary.

WHAT'S IN IT FOR ME?

Ephesus was not a place friendly to the gospel of Jesus Christ—but Paul stayed the course and developed a church there. Whatever your situation, God wants you to stay true to Him.

Galilee, Sea of

NAME/MEANING
Named for its location in the ancient region known as Galilee; also known as Lake Tiberias, Sea of Chinnereth, and Sea of (or Lake) Gennesaret. Today the body of water is also called Kam (or Lake) Kinneret ("Harp") because of its shape.

WHERE IN THE WORLD?
The largest freshwater lake in Israel (thirteen miles long by seven miles wide), the Sea of Galilee is located in the Jordan Rift Valley. The Jordan River flows south from the sea to the Dead Sea.

WHERE IN THE BIBLE?
"But in the future he will honor Galilee of the Gentiles, by the way of the sea, along the Jordan" (Isaiah 9:1 NIV).

"As Jesus walked beside the Sea of Galilee, he saw Simon and his brother Andrew casting a net into the lake, for they were fishermen" (Mark 1:16 NIV).

"Afterward [after the Resurrection] Jesus appeared again to his disciples, by the Sea of Tiberias" (John 21:1 NIV).

WHAT HAPPENED THERE?
Much of Jesus' earthly ministry occurred on or near the shores of the Sea of Galilee, a fact prophesied by the prophet Isaiah. Jesus, who was raised in Galilee, would

call the disciples Peter, Andrew, James, and John, all fishermen, by the Sea of Galilee. Several miracles were also performed there, including the feeding of both the four thousand and the five thousand, and Jesus' walking on the water. Jesus also appeared to His disciples after the Resurrection on the shores of the Galilee, directing them to a miraculous catch of fish and then cooking breakfast. During the time of the Byzantine Empire, the Sea of Galilee lost its importance as the towns around it were abandoned.

WHAT'S UP TODAY?

The first kibbutz was built near Lake Kinneret in the early 1900s, sparking the Zionist movement. Today the lake is the source of most of the drinking water of Israel, as well as a popular tourist destination.

WHAT'S IN IT FOR ME?

Just as Jesus called His disciples along the shores of the Sea of Galilee, He calls for us today. . .if we listen for His voice.

Gethsemane

NAME/MEANING
From the Hebrew *Gath-shemanim*, meaning "Oil Press"

WHERE IN THE WORLD?
While the exact location of Gethsemane is unknown, Gospel accounts place it across the Kidron Brook near the foot of the Mount of Olives. In Bible times, this garden or grove of olive trees was to the east of Jerusalem; now it would be contained within the city limits.

WHERE IN THE BIBLE?
"Then Jesus went with his disciples to a place called Gethsemane, and he said to them, 'Sit here while I go over there and pray'" (Matthew 26:36 NIV).

"Jesus went out as usual to the Mount of Olives, and his disciples followed him. On reaching the place, he said to them, 'Pray that you will not fall into temptation'" (Luke 22:39–40 NIV).

"Jesus left with his disciples and crossed the Kidron Valley. On the other side there was an olive grove, and he and his disciples went into it" (John 18:1 NIV).

WHAT HAPPENED THERE?
In the garden or grove of Gethsemane Jesus prayed to His Father, most notably before His ultimate arrest and crucifixion. It is likely Jesus had come here before to

pray. On the night of His arrest, Jesus was accompanied by all of His disciples except Judas Iscariot, who would arrive later in Gethsemane with a large crowd to betray the Lord. Upon entering the olive grove, Jesus asked three of His disciples—Peter, James, and John—to accompany Him farther. Then Jesus went even deeper into the garden to pray alone. He returned three times to His disciples, only to find them sleeping.

WHAT'S UP TODAY?

The area accepted as Gethsemane is still filled with olive trees and remains a sacred area for Christian pilgrims.

WHAT'S IN IT FOR ME?

As with Peter, James, and John in Gethsemane, remaining vigilant for Jesus can be difficult—but the rewards are great.

Heaven

NAME/MEANING

From the Hebrew *samayim*, meaning "Heaved-up Things" or "The Heights"; from the Greek *ouranos*, meaning "Sky" or "Air"

WHERE IN THE WORLD?

Heaven is not of this world but generally believed to be above the clouds—a world of bliss created by God, not visible from earth.

WHERE IN THE BIBLE?

"In my Father's house are many mansions: if it were not so, I would have told you. I go to prepare a place for you. And if I go and prepare a place for you, I will come again" (John 14:2–3 KJV).

"After the Lord Jesus had spoken to them, he was taken up into heaven and he sat at the right hand of God" (Mark 16:19 NIV).

"But our citizenship is in heaven. And we eagerly await a Savior from there, the Lord Jesus Christ, who. . .will transform our lowly bodies so that they will be like his glorious body" (Philippians 3:20–21 NIV).

"Then I saw a new heaven and a new earth, for the first heaven and the first earth had passed away. . . . 'Now the dwelling of God is with men, and he will live with them'" (Revelation 21:1, 3 NIV).

WHAT HAPPENED THERE?

Heaven is where God the Father and Jesus the Son dwell—and where all who profess faith in Jesus Christ will live after they die physically. After Jesus' resurrection, His disciples witnessed Him ascending into the clouds, to heaven. Heaven is described as a place where there is no evil, no pain, and no sadness—and where, in their new bodies, believers can behold God's face. The Bible speaks of a "new heaven and a new earth" which will occur at the end of the age when all biblical prophecy has come to pass.

WHAT'S UP TODAY?

Heaven, like God, remains unchanged through the ages.

WHAT'S IN IT FOR ME?

If you believe in Jesus as your Savior, you'll go to heaven someday.

Jericho

NAME/MEANING
From the Hebrew *Yareah* or *Yerah*, meaning "Fragrant Place" or "City of the Moon God"

WHERE IN THE WORLD?
Jericho, the ruins and the modern city, are located in the West Bank, on the west side of the Jordan River.

WHERE IN THE BIBLE?
"Then Moses climbed Mount Nebo from the plains of Moab to the top of Pisgah, across from Jericho" (Deuteronomy 34:1 NIV).

"But the Babylonian army pursued them and overtook Zedekiah in the plains of Jericho" (Jeremiah 39:5 NIV).

"At that time Joshua pronounced this solemn oath: 'Cursed before the LORD is the man who undertakes to rebuild this city, Jericho'" (Joshua 6:26 NIV).

"Jesus entered Jericho and was passing through. A man was there by the name of Zacchaeus" (Luke 19:1–2 NIV).

WHAT HAPPENED THERE?
While the first settlement dates to 8000 BC, making Jericho the oldest city in the world, little is known of that culture. On top of Mount Nebo, Moses was shown the city by God. Around 1400 BC, Joshua conquered Jericho

at God's direction after marching around the city for seven days. Later, Joshua cursed those who would try to rebuild the city. Jericho was later sacked and rebuilt by Herod the Great, who constructed a new city two miles from the remains of Joshua's siege (now known as Tell es-Sultan). It was this city that Jesus visited, healing two blind men (one named Bartimaeus) and encountering the tax collector Zacchaeus. In Jesus' parable of the Good Samaritan, the traveler is on his way to Jericho. Jericho would later be conquered by the Muslims.

WHAT'S UP TODAY?
Jericho was captured by Israel during the Six-Day War of 1967. In 1994, Jericho, along with Gaza, was handed over to the Palestinian Authority. After a brief Israeli occupation, Jericho was returned to the Palestinian Authority in March 2005. Since the early twentieth century, Jericho has been the focus of intense archaeological study.

WHAT'S IN IT FOR ME?
While in Jericho, Jesus changed Zacchaeus from a hated tax collector to an honest man. He can change your life for the better, too.

Jerusalem

NAME/MEANING

From the Hebrew *Shalem* or *Salem*, meaning "Legacy of Peace"; also from the Hebrew *Ariel*, meaning "Lion of God"

WHERE IN THE WORLD?

Jerusalem, capital and key city of the state of Israel, is located in the Judean Mountains, between the Mediterranean Sea and the northern edge of the Dead Sea.

WHERE IN THE BIBLE?

"David was thirty years old when he became king, and he reigned forty years. In Hebron he reigned over Judah seven years and six months, and in Jerusalem he reigned over all Israel and Judah thirty-three years" (2 Samuel 5:4–5 NIV).

WHAT HAPPENED THERE?

Throughout its history, Jerusalem, which dates to the fourth millennium BC, has been besieged some forty times and destroyed more than thirty, many of which are chronicled in the Bible. The first mention of the city occurs when Abram met Melchizedek, king of Salem (or Jerusalem) following the "War of the Kings." The Jebusites occupied the city until around 1000 BC, when David wrested control and established Jerusalem as the capital of Judea and Israel. The reign of David's son Solomon in Jerusalem was marked by the building of God's Temple, a feat that took seven years. After Solomon's rule, when the twelve tribes of Israel split into two factions, Jerusalem remained the capital of Judah, the Southern Kingdom. During the Babylonian siege, Nebuchadnezzar II destroyed Jerusalem; Nehemiah records the rebuilding of the city's wall some seventy years later. The Roman era saw Herod the Great installed as the Jewish client king, a period that marked Jesus' triumphal entry into Jerusalem and His crucifixion, resurrection, and ascension. Herod was also responsible for the building of the Temple Mount. Byzantines, Arabs, Crusaders, and Ottoman Turks occupied Jerusalem in the succeeding centuries. In 1922, during a British occupation, a Jewish state was again established by the Balfour Declaration. In 1948, on the heels of Israel's independence, Jerusalem was proclaimed the capital of Israel.

WHAT'S UP TODAY?
Following the Six-Day War of 1967, Israel declared sovereignty over the entire city, including East Jerusalem, considered home to many Palestinians. Despite terror threats and the omnipresent specter of war, Jerusalem remains a thriving metropolis and a holy city to Jews, Christians, and Muslims.

WHAT'S IN IT FOR ME?
God's love for Jerusalem permeates the scriptures. As Psalm 122:6 says, pray for the peace of Jerusalem.

Jordan River

NAME/MEANING
From the Hebrew *Nehar Hayarden*, meaning "Flowing Down"

WHERE IN THE WORLD?
The Jordan River runs for 156 miles from north of the Sea of Galilee (in Israel) to the Dead Sea, where it borders Jordan and the West Bank.

WHERE IN THE BIBLE?
"Lot looked up and saw that the whole plain of the Jordan was well watered, like the garden of the LORD" (Genesis 13:10 NIV).

"So when the people broke camp to cross the Jordan, the priests carrying the ark of the covenant went ahead of them" (Joshua 3:14 NIV).

"So he [Naaman] went down and dipped himself in the Jordan seven times, as the man of God [Elisha] had told him, and his flesh was restored" (2 Kings 5:14 NIV).

"Then Jesus came from Galilee to the Jordan to be baptized by John" (Matthew 3:13 NIV).

What Happened There?

Lot separated from his uncle Abram by settling in the lush Jordan Valley. To the Hebrews, "crossing the Jordan" meant going into the Promised Land. When the people crossed, the waters miraculously parted—as they also did when Elijah, and later, Elisha, struck his cloak on the river. Naaman, a commander of the army of Aram, was cured of his leprosy by dipping himself seven times in the Jordan. In the New Testament, John the Baptist's ministry centered on the Jordan River. Jesus Christ Himself came to be baptized by John in the Jordan.

What's Up Today?

Dams and channels built by neighboring countries in the second half of the twentieth century threaten the ecosystem and future of the Jordan. Only a small area of the Jordan—that reserved for baptisms—has been kept relatively unpolluted.

What's in It for Me?

Like the seekers John the Baptist called to the Jordan, we, too, should repent and ask Jesus to forgive our sins.

Kadesh-Barnea

NAME/MEANING
From the Hebrew *Kadesh*, meaning "Consecrated" and *Barnea*, possibly meaning "Desert of Wandering"; also known simply as Kadesh

WHERE IN THE WORLD?
It is thought that Kadesh-Barnea was located north of the Sinai Peninsula, approximately fifty miles east of the Mediterranean Sea, bordering both the Wilderness of Zin and the Wilderness of Paran.

WHERE IN THE BIBLE?
"They [the twelve spies] came back to Moses and Aaron and the whole Israelite community at Kadesh in the Desert of Paran" (Numbers 13:26 NIV).

"In the first month the whole Israelite community arrived at the Desert of Zin, and they stayed at Kadesh. There Miriam died and was buried" (Numbers 20:1 NIV).

"And so you stayed in Kadesh many days—all the time you spent there" (Deuteronomy 1:46 NIV).

"Joshua subdued them from Kadesh Barnea to Gaza and from the whole region of Goshen to Gibeon" (Joshua 10:41 NIV).

WHAT HAPPENED THERE?

Kadesh-Barnea is first mentioned in the Bible in association with Sarah's servant, Hagar, who fled into the desert and met an angel at a well near Kadesh. The angel told her she should return to Sarah and that she would have a son named Ishmael. During their years of wandering from Egypt to Canaan, the Israelites spent most of their time in Kadesh-Barnea. From Kadesh, Moses first sent twelve spies into the Promised Land—and also put up with the Israelites' grumbling and Korah's rebellion. Moses' sister, Miriam, was buried at Kadesh. When the Israelites complained of a lack of water near Kadesh, Moses, acting on God's instruction, struck the rock and water flowed. After the Israelites entered Canaan, Joshua's men controlled a large swath of land including Kadesh.

WHAT'S UP TODAY?

The exact location of Kadesh-Barnea is unknown.

WHAT'S IN IT FOR ME?

The Israelites' time in Kadesh-Barnea was marked by grumbling and lack of faith—so God made them languish in the desert. God wants you to trust in Him.

Mount Carmel

NAME/MEANING
From the Hebrew *Karmel*, meaning "Vineyard of God" or "Garden Land"

WHERE IN THE WORLD?
Mount Carmel, a headland in the Carmel Mountains, borders the Mediterranean Sea in northern Israel. The city of Haifa sits at the base of the mountains.

WHERE IN THE BIBLE?
" 'Now summon the people from all over Israel to meet me [Elijah] on Mount Carmel. And bring the four hundred and fifty prophets of Baal and the four hundred prophets of Asherah, who eat at Jezebel's table'" (1 Kings 18:19 NIV).

"Your head crowns you like Mount Carmel" (Song of Songs 7:5 NIV).

"So she [the Shunammite woman] set out and came to the man of God at Mount Carmel" (2 Kings 4:25 NIV).

WHAT HAPPENED THERE?
Long revered as a place of great beauty and lush vegetation, Mount Carmel was also regarded as a holy place and sanctuary to ancient civilizations. So it's fitting that the prophet Elijah chose that mount as the site for his confrontation with the prophets of Baal.

In a contest to see whose deity would send rain to the famine-parched land, Elijah's God was the victor—first sending fire to consume a sacrifice that had been doused three times with water. Later, God called Elijah to the top of Mount Carmel where He showed him a cloud in the distance, the harbinger of rain. Elijah's successor, Elisha, also spent time on Mount Carmel and was discovered there by the Shunammite woman after her son died. The Carmelite Order of the Catholic Church was established on Mount Carmel in the twelfth century.

WHAT'S UP TODAY?
Much of the Carmel Mountains are included in the Mount Carmel National Park. The mountains are also home to two Druze villages and a Carmelite monastery.

WHAT'S IN IT FOR ME?
The story of Elijah at Mount Carmel proves there is only one true God, and only one way to eternal life.

Mount Moriah

NAME/MEANING
"Land of the Amorites" or "Provided by Jehovah"

WHERE IN THE WORLD?
Mount Moriah is part of an elongated ridge that extends throughout Jerusalem. Mount Zion is to the west and the Mount of Olives is to the east.

WHERE IN THE BIBLE?
"Then God said, 'Take your son, your only son, Isaac, whom you love, and go to the region of Moriah. Sacrifice him there as a burnt offering'" (Genesis 22:2 NIV).

"Then Solomon began to build the temple of the LORD in Jerusalem on Mount Moriah, where the LORD had appeared to his father David. It was on the threshing floor of Araunah, the Jebusite, the place provided by David" (2 Chronicles 3:1 NIV).

WHAT HAPPENED THERE?
It was on Mount Moriah that God tested Abraham's faith, asking him to sacrifice his long-awaited son with Sarah—Isaac—as an offering. As Abraham was about to kill Isaac, an angel of God stopped him, showing Abraham a ram to sacrifice instead. God's prophecy to Abraham that "on the mountain of the Lord it will be provided" (Genesis 22:14 NIV) has been interpreted as a direct reference to Jesus' sacrifice on the cross

thousands of years later. Mount Moriah was also the site of Araunah the Jebusite's threshing floor, which was purchased by David as the site of the future temple of God, to be constructed by David's son Solomon.

WHAT'S UP TODAY?

Mount Moriah is the site of the Dome of the Rock, a Muslim holy place where the prophet Muhammad was said to be transported to heaven for one night. Though in Israeli territory, the Dome of the Rock is under the full control of the Muslim council—and Jews and Christians are banned from holding services there.

WHAT'S IN IT FOR ME?

Abraham's almost-sacrifice of Isaac on Mount Moriah foreshadowed God's ultimate sacrifice of Jesus for our sins. Through that, we have the hope of eternal life.

Mount of Beatitudes

NAME/MEANING
From the Latin *beatitudo*, meaning "Happiness" (or, in modern English, "Possessing a Feeling of Contentment Not Affected by Physical Circumstances")

WHERE IN THE WORLD?
Although the exact location of the Mount of Beatitudes is unknown, most scholars place it on Mount Eremos, at the northwest corner of the Sea of Galilee, between Capernaum and Gennesaret. The mount overlooks the four-mile-long Plain of Gennesaret.

WHERE IN THE BIBLE?
"Now when he saw the crowds, he went up on a mountainside and sat down. His disciples came to him, and he began to teach them, saying: 'Blessed are the poor in spirit, for theirs is the kingdom of heaven. Blessed are those who mourn, for they will be comforted. Blessed are the meek, for they will inherit the earth. Blessed are those who hunger and thirst for righteousness, for they will be filled. Blessed are the merciful, for they will be shown mercy. Blessed are the pure in heart, for they will see God. Blessed are the peacemakers, for they will be called sons of God. Blessed are those who are persecuted because of righteousness, for theirs is the kingdom of heaven. Blessed are you when people insult you, persecute you and falsely say all kinds of evil against you because of

me. Rejoice and be glad, because great is your reward in heaven'" (Matthew 5:1–12 NIV).

WHAT HAPPENED THERE?
Around AD 30, Jesus delivered what has come to be known as the Beatitudes, the beginning of a longer sermon called the Sermon on the Mount. The Beatitudes are eight to nine qualities (some scholars do not include the last element in verse 11) of those who are blessed by God and who one day will enjoy eternal life.

WHAT'S UP TODAY?
In 1939, the Franciscan Sisters, with the support of Italian leader Benito Mussolini, built a church with octagonal walls on Mount Eremos to commemorate the Beatitudes.

WHAT'S IN IT FOR ME?
From the Mount of Beatitudes, Jesus gave the formula for true happiness—words that are just as true today as they were two thousand years ago.

Mount of Olives (Olivet)

NAME/MEANING
"Place of Olives"

WHERE IN THE WORLD?
The Mount of Olives is part of a mountain ridge located east of Jerusalem, in Israel.

WHERE IN THE BIBLE?
"But David continued up the Mount of Olives, weeping as he went; his head was covered and he was barefoot" (2 Samuel 15:30 NIV).

"On that day his [the Lord's] feet will stand on the Mount of Olives, east of Jerusalem and the Mount of Olives will be split in two from east to west, forming a great valley" (Zechariah 14:4 NIV).

"Each day Jesus was teaching at the temple, and each evening he went out to spend the night on the hill called the Mount of Olives" (Luke 21:37 NIV).

WHAT HAPPENED THERE?
The Mount of Olives was a place of refuge for both King David and Jesus Christ. Fleeing for his life from his son Absalom, David escaped to the mount. Likewise, Jesus spent His nights there, away from the demanding crowds. The Mount of Olives was mentioned as Jesus made His triumphal entry into Jerusalem, and it was

also the site of Jesus' sermon known as the Olivet Discourse, when He revealed signs of His second coming to earth. In his Old Testament book, the prophet Zechariah described a latter-day scene on the Mount of Olives when Jesus returns to reign over the entire earth. Following Jesus' ascension, His disciples returned to Jerusalem after spending time on the Mount of Olives. When Jerusalem was destroyed in AD 70, the Mount of Olives served as a replacement for the demolished temple. Since the third millennium BC, the Mount has been a burial place for more than one hundred fifty thousand Jews, including Zechariah. Because of Zechariah's prophecy, many wish to be buried there—as they believe that will be the first place where Jesus redeems the dead.

WHAT'S UP TODAY?

The Mount of Olives and, in particular, the Jewish cemetery, suffered extensive damage during the 1948 and 1967 military conflicts. When the site was under Jordanian rule, a hotel, gas station, and highway were built using some of the gravestones. Since 1967 when the site was returned to Israeli control, great effort has been made to restore the gravesites. A Russian Orthodox church and the Chapel of the Ascension are now located on the Mount of Olives.

WHAT'S IN IT FOR ME?

As Zechariah's prophecy about the Mount of Olives indicates, be watchful: Jesus *is* coming again!

Mount Sinai

NAME/MEANING
From the Hebrew *Sin-ah*, meaning "Hatred," as in other nations hating the Jewish people; also known as *Har-ha-Elohim*, meaning "The Mountain of God," Mount Horeb, and Gebel Musa (Bedouin name meaning "The Mountain of Moses")

WHERE IN THE WORLD?
The exact location of the biblical Mount Sinai is unknown. From the third century AD, the mount was thought to be in the lower central Sinai Peninsula, in Egypt. Some Bible scholars identify Mount Seir, east of the Gulf of Aqaba, as Sinai, while still others point to locations in northwest Saudi Arabia or to Mount Har Karkom in the Negev.

WHERE IN THE BIBLE?
"Mount Sinai was covered with smoke, because the LORD descended on it in fire" (Exodus 19:18 NIV).

"When the LORD finished speaking to Moses on Mount Sinai, he gave him the two tablets of the Testimony, the tablets of stone inscribed by the finger of God" (Exodus 31:18 NIV).

" 'After forty years had passed, an angel appeared to Moses in the flames of a burning bush in the desert near Mount Sinai' " (Acts 7:30 NIV).

WHAT HAPPENED THERE?

While tending the flocks of his father-in-law, Jethro, near Mount Sinai, Moses encountered a burning bush and received a commission from God—to lead His people out of Egypt. During the Exodus, on God's instruction, Moses struck a rock near the mount, providing water for the grumbling Israelites. On a smoking and quaking Mount Sinai, God gave Moses the Ten Commandments on tablets of stone—instructing the Lord's people in righteous living. Centuries later, Elijah fled the wrath of Queen Jezebel by hiding in a cave on Mount Sinai.

WHAT'S UP TODAY?

Archaeologists continue to search for the true Mount Sinai.

WHAT'S IN IT FOR ME?

The most basic rules for human behavior—the Ten Commandments—came to us from Mount Sinai.

Mount Zion

NAME/MEANING
"Sunny"

WHERE IN THE WORLD?
The modern-day Mount Zion, the highest of seven hills that surround Jerusalem, is located south of the Old City's Armenian Quarter.

WHERE IN THE BIBLE?
"Those who trust in the LORD are like Mount Zion, which cannot be shaken but endures forever" (Psalm 125:1 NIV).

"The king and his men marched to Jerusalem to attack the Jebusites. . . . Nevertheless, David captured the fortress of Zion, the City of David" (2 Samuel 5:6–7 NIV).

" 'For out of Jerusalem will come a remnant, and out of Mount Zion a band of survivors' " (Isaiah 37:32 NIV).

"But you have come to Mount Zion, to the heavenly Jerusalem, the city of the living God" (Hebrews 12:22 NIV).

WHAT HAPPENED THERE?
In the Bible, Mount Zion referred to the original Jebusite fortress that David conquered or to the region where that fortress stood. In time Mount Zion came

to represent Solomon's Temple and the surrounding area. Later, Mount Zion was the site of Herod the Great's palace, and might be the location where Pilate interrogated Jesus. Since the Middle Ages, Mount Zion has referred to a flatter, higher hill that Byzantine pilgrims wrongly imagined as the site of Solomon's Temple.

WHAT'S UP TODAY?

Since 1900, Mount Zion has been the site of Dormitian Abbey, dedicated by Kaiser Wilhelm II and now home to German Catholic monks. On the southeast slope of the mount is a structure that may be the remains of the high priest Caiaphas's house.

WHAT'S IN IT FOR ME?

The word *Zion* often is used to mean "Jerusalem" or "the Promised Land". . .or the place where Jesus will reign when He returns to earth." Can you imagine meeting Jesus face-to-face?

Nazareth

NAME/MEANING
From the Hebrew *Netzer*, meaning "Shoot" or "Branch," or from the Hebrew *Na'zar*, meaning "To Watch"

WHERE IN THE WORLD?
Nazareth is located twenty miles east of the Mediterranean Sea and about fifteen miles west of the Sea of Galilee, in Israel.

WHERE IN THE BIBLE?
"In the sixth month, God sent the angel Gabriel to Nazareth. . .to a virgin pledged to be married to a man named Joseph, a descendant of David" (Luke 1:26–27 NIV).

"He went to Nazareth, where he had been brought up, and on the Sabbath day he went into the synagogue, as was his custom" (Luke 4:16 NIV).

WHAT HAPPENED THERE?
Nazareth, which was settled around the twelfth century BC, remained a small village throughout ancient times, most likely due to the presence of only one spring. Mary and Joseph, Jesus' earthly parents, were from Nazareth, and Jesus spent His boyhood there before moving to Capernaum around age thirty. Jesus returned to Nazareth two times after beginning His ministry—and was rejected by the townspeople on

both occasions. During the first visit, Jesus preached in the synagogue from the book of Isaiah, reading these words: "The Spirit of the Sovereign Lord is on me. . . . He has sent me. . .to proclaim the year of the Lord's favor" (Isaiah 61:1–2 NIV). Afterward the furious people tried to throw Jesus off a cliff. During His second visit, the people questioned Jesus' ability to do miracles, saying, "Isn't this the carpenter?" Jesus was amazed at their lack of faith, saying, "Only in his hometown, among his relatives. . .is a prophet without honor" (Mark 6:4 NIV). In the fourth century AD, Constantine constructed a church in Nazareth as a center for Christian pilgrimages.

WHAT'S UP TODAY?
Due to the efforts of the Franciscans, who have been in Nazareth since the seventeenth century, the city has become the largest Christian center in Israel. Today sixty thousand Israeli Arabs (half Christian, half Muslim) live in relative harmony in Jesus' hometown. In 1966 the Roman Catholic Church constructed the largest church building in the Middle East over the remains of an ancient church where the angel Gabriel may have announced the birth of Jesus to Mary. On the outskirts of the city is an area called "New Nazaret," referring to the ruins of the historic village.

WHAT'S IN IT FOR ME?
To the Nazarenes, Jesus was only the son of a carpenter—but we know He is the Son of God.

Nile River

NAME/MEANING

Modern name comes from the Greek *Neilos*, meaning "River Valley"; originally from the Egyptian *Iteru*, meaning "Great River"

WHERE IN THE WORLD?

The Nile (including the White Nile and Blue Nile)—one of the world's longest rivers—flows through nine countries in eastern Africa, including Egypt. The White Nile begins at Lake Victoria, Uganda, and the Blue Nile at Lake Tana, Ethiopia, with the two rivers joining near Khartoum, in the Sudan. The mouth of the Nile is at the Mediterranean Sea.

WHERE IN THE BIBLE?

"Then Pharaoh said to Joseph, 'In my dream I was standing on the bank of the Nile'" (Genesis 41:17 NIV).

" 'By this you will know that I am the Lord: With the staff that is in my hand I will strike the water of the Nile, and it will be changed into blood'" (Exodus 7:17 NIV).

WHAT HAPPENED THERE?

The Nile was the backbone of ancient Egypt, providing food and water, transportation, and commerce—and also regular floods. Ancient Egyptians believed the Nile was the causeway to the afterlife. In the Old Testament, the Nile figures prominently: Pharaoh's dream of seven fat cows and seven lean cows was set on the banks of the Nile; Pharaoh ordered all baby boys born to Hebrews to be thrown into the Nile; baby Moses was rescued by Pharaoh's daughter after floating in a basket on the Nile; and God sent two plagues on Egypt that centered on the Nile (the river turning to blood and teeming with frogs). Several major and minor prophets invoked the Nile in their writings, predicting the drying up of the great river. During the nineteenth and early twentieth centuries, explorers struggled to find the sources of the White and Blue Nile.

WHAT'S UP TODAY?

As in ancient times, most Egyptians still live in the Nile River Valley. Now, though, since the completion of the Aswan High Dam in 1970, flooding has been reduced and the water harnessed to provide hydroelectricity to the region. In addition to its many functions, the Nile recently became a major source of tourism, as it offers a front-row view of the monuments of ancient Egypt.

WHAT'S IN IT FOR ME?

By the Nile River, Joseph told Pharaoh that only God could interpret the ruler's dreams. Like Joseph, we can do nothing without our heavenly Father.

Nineveh

NAME/MEANING
From *Ninua*, meaning "Habitation of Ninus [Nimrod]"

WHERE IN THE WORLD?
The ruins of Nineveh are located across the Tigris River from the city of Mosul in modern-day Iraq.

WHERE IN THE BIBLE?
"He will stretch out his hand against the north and destroy Assyria, leaving Nineveh utterly desolate and dry as the desert" (Zephaniah 2:13 NIV).

"Jonah obeyed the word of the LORD and went to Nineveh. Now Nineveh was a very important city—a visit required three days" (Jonah 3:3 NIV).

" 'The men of Nineveh will stand up at the judgment with this generation and condemn it; for they repented at the preaching of Jonah, and now one greater than Jonah is here' " (Matthew 12:41 NIV).

WHAT HAPPENED THERE?
Although Nineveh dates to at least 1800 BC, the city did not achieve renown until after its capture by the Assyrians in the fourteenth century BC and, in particular, the reign of King Sennacherib starting in 705 BC. Sennacherib laid out a magnificent city, known for its elaborate palace, canal system, and fifteen gates, each named for

an Assyrian deity. The greatness of Nineveh would be fleeting: By 612 BC, the city was razed and the spoils divided by the Medes and Babylonians. According to the Bible, the city was built by Asshur, a grandson of Noah, during the time of Nimrod. Most prominently, Nineveh, known for its worship of the goddess Ishtar, was where God told the prophet Jonah to preach—which he did, reluctantly, only after being swallowed, then released, by a giant fish. In Jonah's time, the circumference of Nineveh, an important center of commerce due to its location between the Mediterranean Sea and the Indian Ocean, was estimated to be sixty miles.

WHAT'S UP TODAY?
Since the nineteenth century, archaeologists have uncovered a few chambers of Sennacherib's palace and reconstructed five of Nineveh's famous gates.

WHAT'S IN IT FOR ME?
At God's direction and in God's power, Jonah pointed the wicked city of Nineveh to repentance. And God can give you the strength to do what seems impossible, too.

Patmos

NAME/MEANING
Possibly from Latmos, a city in Turkey, or Mount Latmos

WHERE IN THE WORLD?
The Greek island of Patmos is the northernmost of the Dodecanese Islands, located in the Aegean Sea. Patmos is 140 miles (a ten-hour ferry ride) from Athens, Greece.

WHERE IN THE BIBLE?
"I, John, your brother and companion in the suffering and kingdom and patient endurance that are ours in Jesus, was on the island of Patmos because of the word of God and the testimony of Jesus. On the Lord's Day I was in the Spirit, and I heard behind me a loud voice like a trumpet, which said: 'Write on a scroll what you see and send it to the seven churches: to Ephesus, Smyrna, Pergamum, Thyatira, Sardis, Philadelphia and Laodicea'" (Revelation 1:9–11 NIV).

WHAT HAPPENED THERE?
First populated in 500 BC, Patmos came under Roman rule during the second century BC. Neglected by the Romans, the island became a place of banishment for criminals and dissidents—including the apostle John, who was exiled there by the emperor Domitian in AD 95. John received a vision from God concerning the end

times—a vision that became the book of Revelation—while tradition says he was living in a cave (now called the Cave of the Apocalypse) on Patmos. Eighteen months after his exile, John received permission from the Roman emperor to return to Ephesus. In more modern times, Patmos was controlled by Turkey (1523–1912) and Italy, before being ceded to Greece after World War II.

WHAT'S UP TODAY?

Patmos, a small, mountainous, volcanic island with three villages, has become a tourist attraction and destination for Christian pilgrims. The key destination is the seventeenth-century Monastery of St. John, which encloses the Cave of the Apocalypse.

WHAT'S IN IT FOR ME?

John's banishment on Patmos closed him off from society—but opened a window for all time into the future. God uses us where we are right now.

Peniel

NAME/MEANING
"The Face of God" (also spelled Penuel)

WHERE IN THE WORLD?
Peniel was located east of the Jordan River, near a ford of what was then known as the Jabbok River (now called the Zarka). The Zarka begins in present-day Amman, Jordan, and flows north and then west for sixty-five miles.

WHERE IN THE BIBLE?
"So Jacob called the place Peniel, saying, 'It is because I saw God face to face, and yet my life was spared.' The sun rose above him as he passed Peniel, and he was limping because of his hip" (Genesis 32:30–31 NIV).

"From there he [Gideon] went up to Peniel and made the same request of them, but they answered as the men of Succoth had. So he said to the men of Peniel, 'When I return in triumph, I will tear down this tower'" (Judges 8:8–9 NIV).

"Then Jeroboam fortified Shechem in the hill country of Ephraim and lived there. From there he went out and built up Peniel" (1 Kings 12:25 NIV).

What Happened There?

When Jacob was traveling home with his family to Bethel after serving his uncle and father-in-law, Laban, for many years, he camped beside the Jordan River. During the night, he wrestled with a man (who was really God in the flesh) who blessed Jacob by giving him the new name of *Israel*. After the encounter, which left him crippled, Jacob named the place Peniel. The next day, Jacob bowed before his estranged brother, Esau, leading an army of four hundred men, and the two enjoyed a tearful reunion. Years later, when Peniel was a city, Gideon and his three hundred men stopped there to ask for bread before a battle with the Midianites. When the people refused him, Gideon returned to destroy Peniel's tower and kill the men of the city. Years after that, Israel's King Jeroboam I rebuilt Peniel as one of his many sites for idol worship.

What's Up Today?

The actual site of Peniel is unknown.

What's in It for Me?

After Jacob's night at Peniel, God led him all the way home. Have you sensed God's direction for your life?

Persia

NAME/MEANING
From the Farsi *Parsa*, meaning "Above Reproach"

WHERE IN THE WORLD?
Persia is synonymous with the modern country of Iran.

WHERE IN THE BIBLE?
" 'Though we are slaves, our God has not deserted us in our bondage. He has shown us kindness in the sight of the kings of Persia'" (Ezra 9:9 NIV).

"So Daniel prospered during the reign of Darius and the reign of Cyrus the Persian" (Daniel 6:28 NIV).

WHAT HAPPENED THERE?
The Persian Empire, one of the world's great dynasties, came into flower under Cyrus II in 539 BC with the conquest of Babylon—and sputtered out beginning in AD 643. Under Darius I, the Persian Empire enjoyed its greatest years, encompassing Egypt and even parts of Europe, with its administrative center in Susa. These years correspond to events recorded in the Bible: In 539 BC, Cyrus issued a decree allowing Jews to return to Jerusalem (as recorded by Ezra), a decree issued again in 521 BC by Darius. The prophet Daniel, who served Darius, records the king's irrevocable order that his subjects should pray only to him, which resulted in Daniel being thrown into the lions' den for continuing

to pray to God. In 515 BC, the new temple was dedicated in Jerusalem, and Ezra himself returned to Jerusalem in 458 BC. The story of Esther and her bravery to save her people, the Jews, occurred in Susa sometime between 486–465 BC, under the reign of Xerxes. Alexander the Great conquered Persia in 331 BC, followed by conquests by the Greeks, Parthians, and the Arab Caliphate. From AD 1219 to 1500, Genghis Khan and his successors ruled Persia. In the aftermath of World War I, the last Persian monarch, Reza Shah Pahlavi, seized power and in 1935 requested that the nation be called Iran.

WHAT'S UP TODAY?

The year 1979 marked the end of the Pahlavi dynasty and the start of the Islamic Revolution, with the shah fleeing Iran, the seizing of American hostages at the US embassy, and the arrival of the Ayatollah Khomeini. From 1980 to 1988, Iran waged war with Iraq, a conflict finally resolved by the United Nations. The early twenty-first century has seen elevated hostility between Iran and the United States, sparked by rumors of increasing nuclear capability by Iran.

WHAT'S IN IT FOR ME?

God rescued Daniel from a Persian lions' den—and He'll rescue each of us from our sins if we ask.

Red Sea

NAME/MEANING

The name is derived from the Greek *Erythra Thalassa*, meaning "Red Sea" or from the Hebrew *Yam suph*, meaning "Reed Sea." While the water is not red, the name may have been given because of the red-colored cyanobacteria near the water surface or because of the red mountains nearby known as Harei Edom. (Edom is another name for Esau, meaning "Ruddy Complexion.") The name could also refer to Egypt, which borders the sea, a country known as the "Red Land."

WHERE IN THE WORLD?

The Red Sea is a narrow strip of water, twelve hundred miles long, that lies between Africa and the Arabian Peninsula, beginning in Suez and ending at the Bab el-Mandeb Strait.

WHERE IN THE BIBLE?

"So God led the people around by the desert road toward the Red Sea" (Exodus 13:18 NIV).

" 'Pharaoh's chariots and his army he has hurled into the sea. The best of Pharaoh's officers are drowned in the Red Sea'" (Exodus 15:4 NIV).

" 'I will establish your borders from the Red Sea to the Sea of the Philistines, and from the desert to the River'" (Exodus 23:31 NIV).

What Happened There?

The Red Sea is first mentioned in the Bible in connection with the plague of locusts that God, through Moses, brought on Pharaoh. When God lifted the plague, He sent the locusts into the Red Sea. After the night of the first Passover, when all the firstborn sons of the Egyptians were killed, God miraculously separated the waters of the Red Sea, allowing the Israelites to pass over on dry ground. He then caused the waters to flow back over the pursuing Egyptian army. The Red Sea later figured as one of the borders of the Promised Land, which God described to Moses, and as the site of shipbuilding by the wealthy King Solomon. From the fifteenth century to the present, the Red Sea has been used as a channel for trade among Europe, Africa, and Asia, a practice greatly enhanced by the completion of the Suez Canal in 1869. The canal had been envisioned by one of Napoleon's engineers after a frustrated attempt to capture the Red Sea in 1798.

What's Up Today?

The Red Sea, one of the most saline bodies of water in the world, is known for its rich ecosystem, including coral reefs. Where the Israelites once fled for their lives, scientific research and tourism are evident.

What's in It for Me?

The crossing of the Red Sea was a miracle by God, not an act of nature. Nothing is impossible for God

Rome

NAME/MEANING
From the Proto-Indo-European root meaning "river," Rome means "Town on the River"

WHERE IN THE WORLD?
Rome is located near the west coast of central Italy, not far from the Tyrrhenian Sea.

WHERE IN THE BIBLE?
"The following night the Lord stood near Paul and said, 'Take courage! As you have testified about me in Jerusalem, so you must also testify in Rome'" (Acts 23:11 NIV).

"I am obligated both to Greeks and non-Greeks, both to the wise and the foolish. That is why I am so eager to preach the gospel also to you who are at Rome" (Romans 1:14–15 NIV).

WHAT HAPPENED THERE?
The beginnings of Rome can be traced to the eighth century BC. From the Roman Kingdom to the Roman Republic with its Senate (510 BC) to the glory days of the Roman Empire with its legendary Caesars (31 BC–AD 476), Rome has been at the center of world history. For a time, it was the most powerful city in the western world. Following the fall of the empire, Rome became part of the Byzantine Empire before being overrun

by Germanic barbarians. Almost forgotten during the Middle Ages, Rome flourished again during the Renaissance and Baroque periods. In the Bible, Rome is presented as the ultimate authority on earth, whether for levying taxes or deciding the fate of a well-traveled missionary like the apostle Paul. Under Tiberius Caesar Augustus, the second emperor of Rome, a decree was issued that "all the world should be taxed" (Luke 2:1 KJV), thus laying the groundwork for Mary and Joseph's journey to Bethlehem. Tiberius was in his fifteenth year as Caesar when John the Baptist began preaching in the wilderness. Under Claudius, the fourth emperor, Jews were prohibited from living in Rome en masse. Finally, the apostle Paul, as a Roman citizen, appealed to the highest court in the land—Rome—to decide his fate. He died a martyr's death in Rome during Nero's watch in AD 67.

WHAT'S UP TODAY?

Following World War I, Rome and Italy, under the fascist dictatorship of Benito Mussolini, sided with Nazi Germany. In the aftermath of World War II, Italy became a republic, and Rome once again enjoyed a resurgence.

WHAT'S IN IT FOR ME?

Roman citizenship was a much sought-after reward in Bible times. Do we feel the same way about our citizenship in heaven?

Samaria

NAME/MEANING
From the Hebrew *Shemer*, the individual from whom Omri, king of Israel, purchased the site of Samaria

WHERE IN THE WORLD?
Samaria is a mountainous region located in the northern West Bank of Israel. To the east is the Jordan River; to the west, the Carmel Ridge.

WHERE IN THE BIBLE?
"He [Omri] bought the hill of Samaria from Shemer for two talents of silver and built a city on the hill, calling it Samaria, after Shemer" (1 Kings 16:24 NIV).

"When a Samaritan woman came to draw water, Jesus said to her, 'Will you give me a drink?'.... Many of the Samaritans from that town believed in him because of the woman's testimony, 'He told me everything I ever did'" (John 4:7, 39 NIV).

WHAT HAPPENED THERE?
Samaria became the capital of the Northern Kingdom of Israel in the mid-ninth century BC under Omri, and continued throughout the reigns of Ahab to Hoshea. Following the Assyrian conquest in 721 BC, the city was frequently besieged, most notably by the Babylonians and Persians. In 30 BC, Samaria was awarded to Herod the Great, who named it Sebaste. During the time of

Jesus, Samaria was one of three provinces in the area, sandwiched between Judea and Galilee. Because of the religion of the Samaritans—a hybrid of Judaism and paganism—the Samaritans were disdained by the Jews. That attitude gave Jesus' parable of the Good Samaritan and His encounter with the woman at the well special meaning. The apostles Philip, Peter, and John all preached in Samaria with much success. After its destruction by Rome in AD 67, the city of Samaria enjoyed a brief period of grandeur during the Byzantine Empire before being destroyed by an earthquake in AD 551.

WHAT'S UP TODAY?

Samaria is under the jurisdiction of the Palestinian Authority and Israel. Some of Samaria's most beautiful landscapes are protected in the Samaria National Park.

WHAT'S IN IT FOR ME?

Jesus already knew everything about the woman at the well in Samaria—but He still took the time to talk with her. He wants to hear from us today, too.

Siloam, Pool of

NAME/MEANING
From the Hebrew *Siloam*, meaning "Sent" or "Sending"

WHERE IN THE WORLD?
The Pool of Siloam is located just outside the walls of the Old City of Jerusalem, in Israel.

WHERE IN THE BIBLE?
"As he went along, he saw a man blind from birth. His disciples asked him, 'Rabbi, who sinned, this man or his parents, that he was born blind?' 'Neither this man nor his parents sinned,' said Jesus, 'but this happened so that the work of God might be displayed in his life....' Having said this, he spit on the ground, made some mud with the saliva, and put it on the man's eyes. 'Go,' he told him, 'wash in the Pool of Siloam' (this word means Sent). So the man went and washed, and came home seeing" (John 9:1–3, 6–7 NIV).

WHAT HAPPENED THERE?
The Pool of Siloam, constructed during the first century BC, was a freshwater reservoir that served as a gathering place for Jews making pilgrimages to Jerusalem. The pool was fed from water flowing down from Hezekiah's Tunnel. It was at the Pool of Siloam that Jesus healed a man blind from birth, a miracle that provoked great consternation among the Pharisees. After the man was dismissed by the Pharisees, he met Jesus again and

confessed his faith in the Lord. The pool was destroyed around AD 70.

WHAT'S UP TODAY?
In 2004 a team of Israeli archaeologists uncovered what they believe to be the Pool of Siloam where Jesus healed the blind man. (Another pool, thought for centuries to be the Pool of Siloam, was actually built around AD 400–460.) Several steps have been uncovered, leading down to the site of the pool. Further excavation is pending permission from a nearby Greek Orthodox church.

WHAT'S IN IT FOR ME?
After the blind man washed his eyes in the Pool of Siloam, as Jesus said, he could see again. When you love Jesus, you see the world differently.

Sodom and Gomorrah

NAME/MEANING
Sodom comes from the Arabic *Sadama*, meaning "Fortify"; Gomorrah meaning "Be Deep"

WHERE IN THE WORLD?
Sodom and Gomorrah (and three other cities known as the "Cities of the Plain") were located near the southern end of the Dead Sea.

WHERE IN THE BIBLE?
"Then the LORD said, 'The outcry against Sodom and Gomorrah is so great and their sin so grievous that I will go down and see if what they have done is as bad as the outcry that has reached me'" (Genesis 18:20 NIV).

"Then the LORD rained down burning sulfur on Sodom and Gomorrah—from the LORD out of the heavens. Thus he overthrew those cities and the entire plain, including all those living in the cities—and also the vegetation in the land. But Lot's wife looked back, and she became a pillar of salt" (Genesis 19:24–26 NIV).

WHAT HAPPENED THERE?
The kings of Sodom and Gomorrah were once allies of Abraham. But after Abraham's nephew Lot moved to Sodom, the cities became synonymous with wickedness and moral decay. Because God's two angels could not find even ten righteous men in Sodom, God destroyed

Sodom and Gomorrah by raining down burning sulfur—after Lot and his family fled to safety.

WHAT'S UP TODAY?

In 1973 archaeologists uncovered what they believe to be the ruins of Sodom and Gomorrah near what has come to be known as Mount Sodom. Among the ruins were hundreds of sulfur balls. Mount Sodom is also the site of the Dead Sea Works, an industry that extracts Dead Sea minerals. A few springs and two villages lie nearby.

WHAT'S IN IT FOR ME?

Lot seemed to allow the wickedness of Sodom to affect his judgment. Our world will do the same thing to us, unless we read the Bible, attend a good church, and pray to God regularly for guidance.

Ur

NAME/MEANING
Possibly "Light"

WHERE IN THE WORLD?
The ruins of Ur are located in southern Iraq, near the city of Nasiriyah, south of Baghdad.

WHERE IN THE BIBLE?
"Terah became the father of Abram, Nahor and Haran. . . . While his father Terah was still alive, Haran died in Ur of the Chaldeans, in the land of his birth" (Genesis 11:27–28 NIV).

"Terah took his son Abram, his grandson Lot son of Haran, and his daughter-in-law Sarai, the wife of his son Abram, and together they set out from Ur of the Chaldeans to go to Canaan" (Genesis 11:31 NIV).

"He also said to him, 'I am the LORD, who brought you out of Ur of the Chaldeans to give you this land to take possession of it'" (Genesis 15:7 NIV).

WHAT HAPPENED THERE?
One of the most ancient civilizations, Ur was first settled around 4000 BC in what was then Mesopotamia. At the time, the city was set on the Euphrates River near the Persian Gulf. Several dynasties of Sumerians occupied Ur and made it a center of learning and culture.

During the twenty-first century BC, a ziggurat—temple of Nanna, the moon god of the Sumerians—was completed. Abraham, the Old Testament patriarch who was born around 1800 BC, was raised in Ur and directed by God to leave that pagan culture for Canaan. During the sixth century BC, the city was rebuilt by Nebuchadnezzar II as Babylon seized control. By the fourth century BC, because of the changing course of the Euphrates, the city of Ur was abandoned.

WHAT'S UP TODAY?
From the mid-1800s to 1934, archaeologists from the British Museum worked to uncover the ziggurat of Ur. The site has not attracted many visitors due to recent military conflicts in Iraq.

WHAT'S IN IT FOR ME?
Abraham heard God's voice in Ur—and followed the Lord's instructions to move on. We should listen for that same voice.

Scripture Index

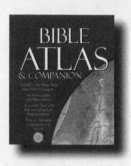